Cromosys Publication

English Speaking and Grammar

NIRANJAN JHA SHOWMAN

Founder - Niranjan Jha Showman

Education and Technology Research Center

Patankar Park, Nallasopara (W), Mumbai. +91-9561450045

Education, Technology, Publication, Healthcare, Newsmedia, Realtor, Filmmaking

www.facebook.com/cromosys

+91-9561450045
Learn Advanced Skills
And Get Job Instantly
GERMAN
Python
FRENCH
C++
SPANISH
Java
ENGLISH
HTML5
RUSSIAN
CSS
JavaScript
Cromosys
Education and Technology Research Center
Nallasopara (W), Mumbai

Learn Web Programming
Demo-Class Free
HTML
CSS
React
JavaScript
Typescript
Bootstrap
Cromosys
20 Years of Experience
Nallasopara (W), Mumbai
+91-9561450045

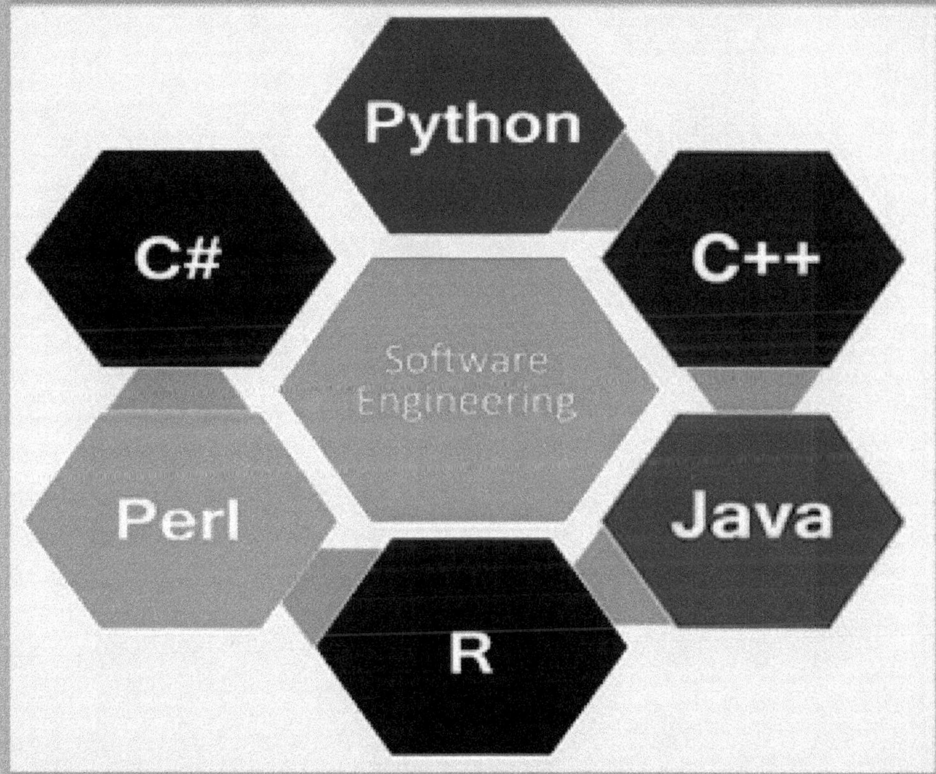
+91-9561450045
Learn Software Engineering
Demo-Class Free
Python
C#
C++
Software
Engineering
Perl
Java
R
Cromosys
20 Years of Experience
Nallasopara (W), Mumbai
+91-9561450045

25 Years of Experience
Learn Visual Multimedia
Animation VFX
Movie Editing
Game Development
Cromosys
+91-9561450045
Education and Technology Research Center
Nallasopara (W), Mumbai
www.facebook.com/cromosys

JOB

Jobs Available
For Candidates Who Know

German
French
Spanish

Vacancy in Germany, France, Spain
For Hospitality, Engineering, IT Sector
With Free Visa, Airfare and Accommodation

Cromosys
Education and Technology Research Centre
Nallasopara (W), Mumbai
+91-9561450045
20 Years of Experience

+91-9561450045
Foreign Languages Institute
German, French, Spanish
Basic and Advanced - All Levels
3 x 6 = 18 Courses
FRANCHISE
Business Offer
Teaching Materials Provided
We have 1 Million Students Globally
Great Income Assured
Global Exposure
Cromosys
20 Years of Experience
Nallasopara (W), Mumbai
+91-9561450045

Cromosys Publication

English Speaking and Grammar

Niranjan Jha Showman

"Education taken with zeal educes to success."
~Niranjan Showman

Preface

Cromosys Publication's "English Speaking and Grammar" book is an optimal quality guide to the beginners as well as advanced learners of English. It is a proven book to gain good knowledge of Spoken English by framing sentences fast and correct. An unmatchable unique book of its kind that guarantees your success has well-explained lessons which are based on my fifteen years of research in linguistic field. The study materials are magnificently powerful to bring you into linguistic light. Since English is accepted as a global language, people around the world have been sharpening their knowledge to be good in it. Sometimes, only working knowledge of it doesn't work, and you feel that there is a lot more to explore. The accurate and profound knowledge of this language, which was considered to be existing only in England and America in past, has influenced zillions of mind today. Therefore, I conceived the idea of making this book a guideline for those who want to be perfect in Written and Spoken English.

The significance of this book is that it is dynamic, systemic and blissful with abundance of pure and perfect set of rules that took a decade of time in preparation. One being immaturely suggested, spend ages in reading literature, watching movies and listening to the audio, which help them to imitate a little but not learn what in actual sense it is. And their never-ending process of Picasso Adventure collects some scattered information which is unworthy to knowledge enhancement. So the aspirants get lost in wilderness. Whether your intention is to travel abroad or plunge deep into your research, you have to be good in English to survive in today's world. Around eight years ago, I went to the USA where I got a chance to get an exclusive training of English. I have been communicating with English-speaking people around the world while managing a team in several call centers, and in part time, I have been teaching this language globally with high exposure. So being able to understand linguistic science, I would like to assure you that the knowledge that you are going to get from this book will definitely sharpen your ability so that you can make your way of success without any hindrance.

After you start the lesson of this book, you don't need to worry about anything but just follow each and everything carefully. Don't procrastinate and never give up. You are going to do beautiful thing for yourself, so be bold and complete all the lessons. The sentence constructions explained in this book is the easiest method I could ever find and that need your practice with effort. The world growing with density has brought enormous opportunity to linguistic talents irrespective of their geographical boundaries. I strongly believe this book is useful for the people working for communication-based industry, media houses, entertainment world, and obviously for those who love English. This book will stand a milestone for you in your journey. You may have seen some other English books or CDs full of conversations and dialogues which the students purchase by mistake. But the students quit learning from those books very soon because they don't find explanation there. So I have designed this book with proper set of rules to make you start your adventure sitting at home beginning with real basic.

Cromosys, our education and technology research center, saving human efforts from being wasted, is dedicated to teach you this language as good as possible. The world growing with density has brought enormous opportunity to foreign language speakers irrespective of their geographical boundaries. Having been teaching this language from several years, I have come across numerous unique rules which I have elaborated and explained in this book. Our path-breaking pioneer training institute, Cromosys, is committed to enlightening human mind with educational endeavors, and we are doing the same from fifteen successful years. I believe I have done all that I could to make this book useful to you, and not only hopeful but I am sure that your success is in your hand now because this book will take you miles ahead in your expectation. We always respect the views and comments of readers, so for any communication with regards to assistance, enquiry or collaboration, we are always at your reach as it helps us improve our ability.

Niranjan Jha Showman
Trainer, Author, Physician, Entrepreneur, Filmmaker, Activist
Founder of Cromosys Corporation
facebook.com/cromosys
+91-9561450045
cromosys@yahoo.com
Nallasopara (W), Mumbai, India

My other books: -
English Word Power
English Voice Accent and Pronunciation
Teach Yourself German
Teach Yourself French
Teach Yourself Spanish
Be millionaire like me
Dynamic Grammar of English
Teach Yourself HTML5
Teach Yourself 3ds Max
Teach Yourself Autodesk Maya

Cromosys Corporation
Education and Technology Research Center
Education, Technology, Publication, Healthcare, Realtor, Filmmaking
facebook.com/cromosys
+91-9561450045
cromosys@yahoo.com
Nallasopara (W), Mumbai, India

About the Author

Niranjan Jha Showman
Trainer, Author, Physician, Entrepreneur, Filmmaker, Activist

Niranjan Jha Showman is a Language Scientist and Technical Researcher. He is the Award Winning author of more than fifty educational and fictional books at Amazon. He is one of the great-grandsons of the first President of India Dr. Rajendra Prasad. He is a Public Figure, and the globally - renowned Languages Trainer of French, Spanish, and German from past twenty years. Niranjan Jha Showman is an Entrepreneur and also works as a Filmmaker in India. Being the founder and owner of Cromosys Corporation - a company located in Mumbai, India, his company is excelling in the fields of Education, Technology, Publication, Newsmedia, Realtors, Banking, and Cinemascope from past fifteen years.

Niranjan Jha Showman's good-seller educational books and novels are appreciated worldwide. He has more than one million eBook buyers online, and more than one million learners are connected to him globally. One of his novels is critically acclaimed. He is the trainer of French, Spanish, German, English Voice and Accent, and Advanced Computer Education. He is also a political activist in India.

Niranjan Jha Showman is the man who came from rags to riches, he who knows how to turn the table, and he, whom you call the man of Midas-touch. He has observed lives from the Pandora of monkeys to the sanctuary of monks, not only down-to-earth but down-to-grave. He is a B. Com. graduate, and B. Ed. from Delhi University, and diploma holder in French, Spanish and German from America. You can watch his songs, movies, educational videos and many more things by typing "Niranjan Jha Showman" in Google.

Niranjan Jha Showman
+91-9561450045
cromosys@yahoo.com
Mumbai, India
facebook.com/cromosys

Statutory

This book with its content is the registered property of the author Niranjan Jha Showman.
The author and his Cromosys Publication holds all necessary rights of this book.
The copyright certificate of this book is attached at the end of this book.

Modals

The word that describes the mood of a verb is called modal.

Can

Definition: The modal can explains the capacity or ability of the doer in present.

Rule: Subject + can + verb 1st + object

Affirmative

    I can do this work.
    (It means: I am able to do this work, or I have the capacity to do this work)
    You can meet him.
    We can reach there.
    She can speak French.
    They can buy a car.

Negative

    He can not help me.
    The Children can not go there.
    You can not talk to him.
    We can not cheat him.
    Rita can not sing a song.

Interrogative

    Can she write a letter?
    Can you not answer these questions?
    How can we meet him?
    Why can you not speak French?
    What can we say now?

Exercise
Change these sentences into negative and interrogative forms.

We can call him here. The students can pass this exam. They can help poor. My brother can speak Spanish. The teacher can teach science. I can answer these questions. It can be true.

Note: **Subject** – one who does a work
           Verb – the action or the work
           Object – the thing which is affected by the work or action

V 1st = go, V 2nd = went, V 3rd = gone, V 4th = going, V 5th = goes

Could

Definition: The modal could describes the capacity of past.

Rule: Sub + could + verb 1st + object

Affirmative

    We could reach there on time.
    (It means: We succeeded in reaching there on time)
    She could speak French with me.
    I could do this work properly.
    She could help me with money.
    He could play the game.
    Your friend could pass the exam.

Negative

    The Children could not go there.
    You could not talk to him.
    He could not explain us anything.
    You could not answer these questions.
    The thief could not open the lock.
    My neighbor could not buy a car.

Interrogative

    Could she help you?
    Could you not buy the book?
    Why could he not meet me?
    How could you do this work?
    Where could she go from there?
    What could Martin find there?
    When could they blow the siren?

Alert:

He can play cricket. (Present Capacity)
He could play cricket. (Past Capacity)

Exercise
Change these sentences into negative and interrogative forms.

She could switch on the computer. The children could play football. He could win the race. My brother could speak Spanish. Rita could marry Peter. I could answer these questions. Her brother could become a doctor. I could check his work. They could jump over the wall. We could win the match. She could prepare the food.

Should

It describes the duty or obligation of the doer.

Rule: Sub + should + verb 1st + object

Affirmative

    He should speak French with me.
    (It means: It is his duty or obligation to speak French)
    I should do this work today.
    He should help me with money.
    We should reach there on time.
    We should respect our elders.
    Jane should work hard for the test.

Negative

    The children should not go there.
    We should not buy this book.
    They should not do this work.
    You should not ask him any question.
    I should take care of my health.
    I should motivate the people.

Interrogative

    Should you compete with him?
    Should I not consult the doctor?
    How should we solve this problem?
    What should I tell him?
    Where should they go now?
    How should you explain him?

Alert:

Shall I go? (A formal request asking permission)
Should I go? (A request showing duty)
Can I go? (A request showing capacity)
May I go? (A request seeking to be allowed to go)

He can play. (Present Capacity)
He could play. (Past Capacity)
He should play cricket. (Duty)
He ought to play. (Moral Duty: Old usage)

Exercise
Change these sentences into negative and interrogative forms.

He should reach school on time. You should listen to his problem. I should give him a chance. They should forgive him. The children should play football. My brother should speak Spanish. Her brother should go to America.

Would

It describes the possibility of past-action.

Rule: Sub + would + verb 1st + object

Affirmative

Your brother would teach you.
(It means: You think it was the possibility that his brother taught him, but not sure)
She would like you very much.
You would improve your skills.
They would strengthen their knowledge.
He would invite you for dinner.
You would trust your neighbors.

Negative

The children would not go there.
You would not talk to him.
They would not learn English properly.
He would care for his future.
The patient would not take the medicine.
The student would not value study.

Interrogative

Would she work hard?
Would the people not read novels?
Why would your brother not drink coffee?
How would he manage his business?
Where would she live in England?
What would they have in breakfast?

Alert:

He can play cricket. (Present Capacity)
He could play cricket. (Past Capacity)
He should play cricket. (Duty)
He would play cricket. (Past Possibility)

Exercise
Change these sentences into negative and interrogative forms.

They would know the truth. He would respect his senior. The people would struggle a lot. Abraham would love Sophia. The king would hide the fact. The teacher would encourage the children. The police would understand the reality.

May

It is used to show the possibility of present.

Rule: Sub + may + verb 1st + object

Affirmative

The teacher may teacher French today.
(It means: The teacher will possibly teach – not surely)
She may appear for exam.
The students may come late.
He may ask you difficult questions.
You may remove this tag.
I may resolve this matter.

Negative

The doctor may not come to the hospital.
You may not convince the financer.
She may not pity you.
The king may not punish the culprit.
Your brother may not understand the problem.
The child may not answer the call.

Interrogative

May he work hard?
May she become ill?
May the teacher not explain the module?
May Sophia become a professor?
May the performer play a stunt?
How may she come here now?
What may you hide from him?

Alert:

He may play cricket. (Present Possibility)
He can play cricket. (Present Capacity)
He might play cricket. (Very less possibility in present)

Exercise

Change these sentences into negative and interrogative forms.

Your sister may sing well. They may fix this issue. He may survive the attack. The manager may come for visit. His friend may buy a car. They all may pass this exam. You may convince him for this.

Have to

It describes the compulsion of present, as if something is compulsory to be done.

Rule: Sub + have to / has to + verb 1st + object

Note: I, we, you, they, plural noun = have to
He, she, it, name, singular noun = has to

Affirmative

      I have to do this work.
      (It means: It is compulsory for me to do this work)
      She has to marry you this year.
      The children have to watch this movie.
      My brother has to complete this work.
      The stranger has to show his identity.
      The labor has the lift up the baggage.

Negative

      We have not to say anything. (Old usage)
      We do not have to say anything. (New usage)
      She has not to learn computer.
      She does not have to learn computer.
      The teacher has not to ask him any question.
      The people have not to support terrorism.

Interrogative

      Have you to write a book? (Old usage)
      Do you have to write a book? (New usage)
      Have you not to inform your senior?
      Why has the child not to play in the ground?
      When has he to meet his friends?
      What have you to have in lunch?
      Who has to risk his life?

Exercise

Change these sentences into negative and interrogative forms.

He has to buy a new car. They have to know the truth. The people have to struggle a lot for freedom. Jenifer has to marry Justin. The king has to hide the fact. Your brother has to understand the reality. The people have to support revolution.

Had to
It describes the compulsion of past, as if something was compulsory to be done.

Rule: Sub + had to + verb 1st + object

Affirmative
>She had to become a doctor.
>*(Meaning 1: It was compulsory for her to become a doctor – not sure what happened)*
>*(Meaning 2: It was compulsory for her to become a doctor, so she became)*
>My friend had to visit Australia.
>His wife had to deliver a child.
>I had to concentrate on my study.
>The government had to act sooner.

Negative
>She had not to change the lock. (Old usage)
>She did not have to change the lock. (New usage)
>I had not to shift my luggage there.
>I did not have to shift my luggage there.
>The teacher had not to explain the things in detail.
>You had not to bring the newspaper.

Interrogative
>Had you to watch this movie? (Old usage)
>Did you have to watch this movie? (New usage)
>Had she not to consult the doctor?
>Did she not have to consult the doctor?
>Why had the child to play piano?
>What had you to have in dinner?
>What did you have to have in dinner?
>What work had to finish first?

Alert:
They have to play cricket. (Present Compulsion)
They had to play cricket. (Past Compulsion)

Exercise
Change these sentences into negative and interrogative forms.

My friend had to build a house. She had to buy a new car. They had to find the culprit. The people had to try their best. India had to win this match. You had to remain patient. The government had to reveal the fact.

Used to
It describes past-habitual action.

Rule: Sub + used to + verb 1st + object

Affirmative
He used to work hard.
(It means: He did hard work as a habit in past)
She used to study mathematics.
(It means: She studied mathematics as a habit in past)
I used to help him a lot.
The children used to drink coffee daily.
We used to remain alert.

Negative
The teacher used not to teach him properly. (Old usage)
The teacher did not use to teach him properly. (New usage)
The people used not to worry about anything.
The people did not use to worry about anything.
We used not to involve in dispute.
The government used not to support industries.

Interrogative
Used he to take money from you? (Old usage)
Did he use to take money from you? (New usage)
Used you to read scriptures?
Did you use to read scriptures?
Why used she to spend money lavishly?
What used you to do in England?
What time they used to watch movies?

Alert:
I used to play. (Past habitual action)
I played. (Simple Past Tense)
~~I use to play.~~ (Wrong sentence)

Exercise

Change these sentences into negative and interrogative forms.

She used to learn computer. I used to give her advices. They used to make money illegally. My friend used to watch cricket match. The teacher used to teach them properly. We used to doubt his honesty. The king used to be very brave.

Need to
This modal shows the necessity in present time.

Rule: Sub + need to / must + verb 1st + object

Affirmative
      I need to call him.
      (It means: It is necessary to call him)
      I must call him.
      (It means: It is urgent to call him)
      He needs to work hard.
      You need to be smart.
      The children need to obtain good marks.

Negative
      The people need not to worry about it. (Old usage)
      The people do not need to worry about it. (New usage)
      The people must not worry about it. (Same meaning as above)
      You need not to escape from here.
      You do not need to escape from here.
      You must not escape from here.
      The politicians need not to make false promises.

Interrogative
      Need you to say something? (Old usage)
      Do you need to say something? (New usage)
      Must you say something? (Same meaning as above)
      Why you need to go there?
      Why do you need to go there?
      What she needs to write here?
      What does she need to write here?

Alert:
I need to go. (Necessity)
I must go. (Urgency)
I should go. (Duty)
I have to go. (Compulsion)
I am to go. (Ready State)
I am about to go. (Ready State)

Exercise
Change these sentences into negative and interrogative forms.

They need to learn technologies. She needs to make haste. I need to be here tonight. You need to keep eyes on them. They need to submit the report. The company needs to gain profit. The businessmen need to incur loss.

Tense

Present Indefinite
This tense is used to shows that you do the work in present with indefinite schedule of time.

Rule: Sub + v1 / v5 + object

Note: v1=go, v2=went, v3=gone, v4=going, v5=goes
I, we, you, they, plural noun = v1
He, she, it, singular noun = v5

Affirmative
I play cricket.
You sing songs.
She likes you very much.
They come here daily.
We read this newspaper.
He collects information.

Negative
You do not help him.
She does not speak French.
The people do not know the truth.
I do not appreciate this.
My brother does not like coffee.
He does not waste time.

Interrogative
Do you live in America?
Does she play guitar?
Do they not reach office on time?
What do you know about it?
Why does she not marry you?
Why nobody knows the truth?

Exercise

Change these sentences into negative and interrogative forms.

He speaks German. You drive a car. She likes singing. They advise me. She motivates people. The farmer ploughs the fields. My brother teaches music.

Present Continuous
This tense is used to shows that you are continuously doing the work in present.

Rule: Sub + is / am / are + v4 + object

Note: I = am
          You, we, they, plural noun = are
          He, she, it, singular noun = is

Affirmative
          The children are watching a movie.
          You are reading a book.
          She is calling you there.
          They are coming here today.
          The teacher is teaching mathematics.
          We are feeling cold.

Negative
          I am not doing this work.
          She is not giving him money.
          Your brother is not going to Australia.
          The children are not making noise.
          We are not expecting any benefits.
          The patient is not recovering from the disease.

Interrogative
          Are you selling this watch?
          Is he not learning computer?
          Why are you sending them market?
          What is she doing there?
          When are they reaching office?
          What medicine are you taking this week?
          They are reaching the station in next hour.

Exercise

Change these sentences into negative and interrogative forms.

You are driving a car. The teacher is speaking Spanish. They are talking to him. I am asking you a question. She is calling me. You are doing this work. The child is playing with toys.

Present Perfect

It is used to show that you have done the work completely.

Rule: Sub + have / has + v3 + object

Note: I, we, you, they, plural noun = have
          He, she, it, singular noun = has

Affirmative

    I have bought the book.
    We have given him money.
    She has reached England.
    India has won the match.
    The children have done the work.
    She has understood everything

Negative

    They have not watched the movie.
    He has not sung a song.
    Her sister has not become a doctor.
    The painter has not painted the wall.
    I have not reached there.
    The people have not become rich.

Interrogative

    Have you explained him everything?
    Has the lyricist written a song?
    Have the labors not done the work?
    What have you seen there?
    Why has the boss not given her salary?
    Have you not decided anything yet?

Exercise

Change these sentences into negative and interrogative forms.

They have understood the reality. I have told him everything. The child has broken the plate. We have made a plan. She has achieved success. You have broken your promise. My brother has joined army.

Present Perfect Continuous

This tense describes that you have been doing the work for a long period of time.

Rule: Sub + have been / has been + v4 + object

Note: Point of time (Monday, 4 o'clock, 1985) = since
         Period of time (2 days, 1 week, 5 years) = for

Affirmative
         I have been teaching for ten years.
         She has been writing a book since Monday.
         The teacher has been giving them assignment for a week.
         We have been talking to him for half an hour.
         They have been working on this plan for years.
         The king has been fighting wars for years.

Negative
         They have not been watching movies since afternoon.
         She has not been singing a song since morning.
         We have not been seeing anything unusual here.
         The child has not been improving for past two years.
         They have not been disobeying him.
         The soldiers have not been going through the training.

Interrogative
         Has he been looking at you for a while?
         Have the people been tolerating injustice?
         Why have you been trying this number for hours?
         What have you been expecting from him?
         Why has he been behaving so rudely?
         What has been keeping you there for years?
         What have the people been learning since ages?

Exercise

Change these sentences into negative and interrogative forms.

They have been coloring walls for months. She has been studying in England for years. India has been suffering from corruption for decades. Your brother has been looking for you. She has been thinking so much these days. You have been underestimating his power. Japan has been witnessing earthquakes for years.

Past Indefinite

It is used to show that you did the work in past.

Rule: Sub + v2 + object

Affirmative

     He bought the toys.
     I gave him money.
     They encouraged the people.
     We saw everything in place.
     She became a professor.
     He proclaimed victory.

Negative

     I did not know him. (did + v1)
     She did not meet me.
     We did not promise him anything.
     The children did not understand the lesson.
     The doctor did not cure the patient.
     The police did not arrest him.

Interrogative

     Did you forgive him?
     Did she not like you?
     What did you decide for your career?
     When did they reach their destination?
     How did you recognize him?
     Why did the manager not appoint a clerk?

Alert

I called him. (A long time ago)
I have called him. (Just now)

Exercise

Change these sentences into negative and interrogative forms.

I asked him a question. They dropped the plan. He appreciated my work. She surprised me. The train reached on time. I saved his life. She revealed a secret.

Past Continuous

This tense describes that the work was being continuously done in past.

Rule: Sub + was / were + v4 + object

Note: I, he, she, it, singular noun = was
          You, we, they, plural noun = were

Affirmative

          The child was drinking milk.
          I was working on computer.
          Both of them were taking tea.
          Many of us were getting tired.
          It was raining heavily.
          He was begging for life.

Negative

          She was not taking any decision.
          You were not making him angry.
          The children were not studying properly.
          It was not frightening him.
          They were not expecting anything.
          The people were not living for bread only.

Interrogative

          Was he drawing on the paper?
          Were you not solving the problems?
          Who was making him angry?
          Why was she not telling anything?
          How was your brother preparing for exam?
          What time were you taking the exam?

Exercise

Change these sentences into negative and interrogative forms.

The shopkeeper was selling goods. The train was moving very fast. I was expecting him to come. He was seeking help from somebody. They were traveling by bus. You were giving him the hint. She was going to start speaking.

Past Perfect

It describes that you had done the work already in past.

Rule: Sub + had + v3 + object

Affirmative

>   She had written the lyric.
>   The children had reached market.
>   The teacher had taught French.
>   I had informed him everything.
>   She had proved her honesty.
>   They had got sick.

Negative

>   I had not received your money.
>   She had not got so much cold before.
>   They had not submitted their applications.
>   The government had not been kind to the citizen.
>   I had not felt so hungry before.
>   It had not rained for two years.

Interrogative

>   Had the management taken the risk?
>   Had you had your dinner?
>   Had she withdrawn her money?
>   Why had they left the city?
>   Why had you been there?
>   What had they decided till then?

Exercise

Change these sentences into negative and interrogative forms.

The king had won the battle. The editor had published the news. She had played the trick. They had decided their way. My brother had prepared for exam. She had already been married. The food had gone cold.

Past Perfect Continuous
This tense shows that you had been doing the work for a long period of time in past.

Rule: Sub + had + been + v4 + object

Affirmative
We had been talking to him for half an hour.
They had been working on this plan for years.
I had been teaching for ten years.
She had been writing a book since Monday.
The teacher had been giving assignments for a week.
The trainer had been explaining everything in detail.

Negative
We had not been seeing anything unusual here.
The child had not been improving for past two years.
They had not been watching movies since afternoon.
She had not been singing a song since morning.
They had not been disobeying him.
The citizen had not been revolting since independence.

Interrogative
Had he been looking at you for a while?
Had the people been tolerating injustice?
Why had he been behaving so rudely with you?
Why had you been trying this number for hours?
What had you been expecting from him?
Who had been leading the nation?

Exercise

Change these sentences into negative and interrogative forms.

The shopkeepers had been selling goods since morning. The train had been playing since 3 o'clock. They had been coloring walls for months. She had been studying in England for years. India had been suffering from corruption for decades. She had been thinking so much these days. She had been speaking on the topic for 10 minutes.

Future Indefinite

It is used to show that you will do the work in future.

Rule: Sub + will + v1 + object

Note: In new English the use of shall is generally avoided.

Affirmative

> She will be happy for this.
> I will give him money.
> He will buy the toys.
> They will encourage the people.
> We will wait for the judgment.
> Her sister will become a professor.

Negative

> She will not meet me.
> I will not recognize him.
> We will not promise him anything.
> The children will not understand the lesson.
> The doctor will not cure the patient.
> The artist will not imagine anything new.
> The glass will not break automatically.

Interrogative

> Will they play a trick?
> Will the government not support poor?
> How will you forgive him?
> When will they reach their destination?
> What will you get from it?
> Who will ask him this question?
> Which work will you do first?

Exercise

Change these sentences into negative and interrogative forms.

He will get angry. I will ask him a question. They will drop the plan. The train will not halt here. The bus will reach on time. It will get over. There will be some problem. The teacher will come on time. The director will get some idea. They will sustain the relationship.

Future Continuous

This tense describes that you will be continuously doing the work in future.

Rule: Sub + will be + v4 + object

Affirmative

    We will be waiting for shower.
    The child will be drinking milk.
    I will be working on computer.
    Both of them will be taking tea.
    Many of us will be getting tired.
    It will be raining heavily.
    The duo will be enjoying full night.

Negative

    The singer will not be singing all day.
    She will not be taking any decision.
    You will not be making him angry.
    The children will not be studying properly.
    It will not be frightening him.
    They will not be expecting anything.
    You will not be managing this team anymore.

Interrogative

    Will he be drawing on the paper?
    Will you not be solving the problems?
    Who will be making him angry?
    Why will she be telling anything?
    How will your brother be preparing for exam?
    What will be giving us problems?
    What work will be availing more profits?

Exercise

Change these sentences into negative and interrogative forms.

You will be having some idea. She will be looking strange. You will be solving problems. He will be making giving you clues. You brother will be preparing for exam. They will be starting the project. It will be getting darker.

Future Perfect

This tense shows that you will have done the work completely in future.

Rule: Sub + will have + v3 + object

Affirmative

    The teacher will have taught French.
    I will have informed him everything.
    She will have written the lyric.
    The children will have reached market.
    She will have proved her honesty.
    We will have learnt Spanish.

Negative

    She will not have got success.
    They will not have submitted their applications.
    The government will not have been kind to the citizen.
    I will not have done anything.
    It will not have happened.
    The king will not have taken any decision.

Interrogative

    Will you have had your dinner?
    WIll she have withdrawn her money?
    Why will they have left the city?
    Why will you have been there?
    What will they have decided by then?
    How will we have secured our future?

Alert

I will play. (will do in future)
I will have played. (will finished playing in future)

Exercise

Change these sentences into negative and interrogative forms.

They will have accepted his proposal. The soldiers will have won the war. She will have shown the detail. They will have decided their way. My brother will have passed the exam. You will have married her. It will have destroyed everything.

Future Perfect Continuous

This tense describes that you will be doing something continuously for a long period of time.

Rule: Sub + will have + been + v4 + object

Note: In Future Perfect Continuous tense, instead of since or for, only *from* is used.

Affirmative

I will have been teaching them from two hours.
She will have been writing a book from Monday.
The teacher will have been giving assignments from next week.
We will have been talking to him from half an hour.
They will have been working on this plan for years.
She will have been saving money.

Negative

They will not have been watching movies from afternoon.
She will not have been singing a song from morning.
We will not have been seeing anything unusual here.
The child will not have been improving from next year.
I will have been setting targets from tomorrow.
They will not have been educating people.

Interrogative

Will he have been looking for you?
Will the people have been tolerating injustice?
Why will you have been trying this number from hours?
What will you have been expecting from him?
Why will she have been learning so much?
How will they have been living there?

Exercise

Change these sentences into negative and interrogative forms.

The child will have been playing football from morning. The government will have been giving loans to the people. They will have been coloring walls from months. She will have been studying in England from years. I will have been narrating the stories. You will have been doing your homework. The people will have been demanding for election.

Advanced Modals

Will have to
It describes that the work will be done with compulsion in future.

Hint: Future + Compulsion
Rule: Sub + will have to + verb 1st + object

Affirmative
> You will have to learn Spanish.
> *(It means: It will be compulsory for you to learn Spanish in future)*
> She will have to take a decision.
> We will have to go there by car.
> I will have to find out the truth.
> The businessman will have to launch new products.

Negative
> He will not have to go for the test.
> The people will not have to worry about anything.
> She will not have to make haste.
> You will not have to work so hard.
> They will not have to involve in dispute.

Interrogative
> Will he have to spend his money?
> Will they not have to wait for the night?
> Why will you have to regret for that?
> How will I have the tackle the problem?
> When will I have to see him off?

Alert:
They have to play cricket. (Present Compulsion)
They had to play cricket. (Past Compulsion)
They will have to play cricket. (Future Compulsion)

Exercise

Change these sentences into negative and interrogative forms.

You will have to rush to the station. I will have to give him some money. The child will have to learn a few words. She will have to know everything. You neighbor will have to pay the bill. You will have to count the number. She will have to stay calm.

Would have to
It describes that the work would possibly be done in past with compulsion.

Hint: Past Possibility + Compulsion
Rule: Sub + would have to + verb 1st + object

Affirmative
>She would have to meet you daily.
>*(It means: You assume that she possibly met with compulsion)*
>The people would have to get up early in the morning.
>They would have to buy gifts for festivals.
>You would have to drink coffee everyday.
>The teacher would have to narrate the stories.

Negative
>The children would not have to learn grammar.
>He would not have to wait for the bus.
>You would not have to worry about anything.
>She would not have to reveal the secrets.
>They would not have to learn a new language.

Interrogative
>Would they have to wait for the result?
>Would she have to show her identity card?
>Why would he have to make presentations?
>Would they have to reach home on time?
>Would the officer have to be strict in the office?

Alert:
You have to go. (Present Compulsion)
You will have to go. (Future Compulsion)
You would have to go. (Past Possibility + Compulsion)

Exercise

Change these sentences into negative and interrogative forms.

You would have to ask for money. She would have to have her dinner late. They would have to check all the staffs. The child would have to be alert. The priest would have to console the people. He would have to inform everything to his parents. Her sister would have to buy the medicines.

May have to
It describes that you possibly have to do something.

Hint: Possibility + Compulsion
Rule: Sub + may have to + verb 1st + object

Affirmative
>He may have to admit his mistake.
>*(It means: It is possible that he has to admit his mistake)*
>You may have to accept his proposal.
>They may have to buy a new flat.
>I may have to migrate to England.
>The researcher may have to change his opinion.
>She <u>might</u> have to live there. (Might = less possibility)

Negative
>The government may not have to change the rule.
>The people may not have to face the problem.
>You may not have to make a choice.
>She may not have to struggle so lot.
>The party may not have to fight for election.

Interrogative
>May he have to give up his work?
>May the king have to quit war?
>Why may he have to spend his money?
>May the child have to stay alone?
>What may he have to do next?

Alert:
She will have to sing. (Future Compulsion)
She would have to sing. (Past Possibility + Compulsion)
She may have to sing. (Present Possibility + Compulsion)
She might have to sing. (Present Less Possibility + Compulsion)
She must have to sing. (Urgency + Compulsion)
She should have to sing. (Duty + Compulsion)

Exercise

Change these sentences into negative and interrogative forms.

You may have to meditate in the morning. She may have to announce her marriage. He may have to learn pronunciation. The child may have to stay awake. The report may have to publish this news. This kingdom may have to see a fall. He may have to accept defeat.

Having to
It is used to show that you are compulsorily doing the work in continuation.

Hint: Compulsion + Continuity
Rule: Sub + is/am/are + having to + verb 1st + object

Note: I = am
You, we, they, plural noun = are
He, she, it, name, singular noun = is

Affirmative
I am having to learn German.
(It means: I am continuously learning German as it is compulsory for me)
The child is having to work hard.
She is having to remain awake all nights.
The president is having to consult the advisors.
We are having to work in the night.

Negative
The students are not having to memorize anything.
You are not having to read so many books.
The child is not having to learn music.
She is not having to work on computer.
I am not having to consult any doctor.

Interrogative
Are you having to read newspapers?
Is she having to learn a new language?
Why am I having to face so many challenges?
Are you not having to exercise daily?
Is he not having to take the medicine?

Alert:
We have to learn. (Present Compulsion)
We are having to learn. (Present Continuous Compulsion)
We are learning. (Present Continuous Tense)
We have been learning. (Present Perfect Continuous Tense)
We have learnt. (Present Perfect Tense)
We are going to learn. (Task Scheduled)
We are to have learnt. (Infinitive To: They are ready to be gone)

Exercise
Change these sentences into negative and interrogative forms.

He is having to read scriptures. The people are having to bathe in the river. The man is having to live in jungle. You are having to learn new customs. She is having to encourage villagers. The students are having to work hard this year. I am having to have juice in the morning.

Could have + V³

It describes that you were capable to do the work but you did not do.

Hint: Past Capability + Work not done
Rule: Sub + could have + v3 + object

Affirmative
    I could have done this work.
    (It means: I was capable to do the work but I did not do)
    She could have passed the exam.
    (It means: She was able to pass the exam but she did not pass)
    He could have learnt Russian.
    (It means: He was able to learn Russian but he did not learn)
    The police could have arrested him.
    (It means: The police was capable to arrest him but they did not arrest)

Negative
    You could not have watched the movie.
    (It means: You were not able to watch the movie but you watched it)
    She could not have answered this question.
    (It means: She was not able to answer the question but she answered)
    The child could not have drunk milk.
    (It means: The child was not able to drink the milk but he drank)
    The teacher could not have explained him.
    (It means: The teacher was not able to explain but he explained)

Interrogative
    Could he have played cricket?
    (It means: Was he able to play cricket that he did not play?)
    Could you not have given him money?
    (It means: Were you not able to give him money that you gave now?)
    Why could she not have done this work?
    (It means: Why was she not able to do the work before that she did now?)
    When could we have met him?
    (It means: When were we able to meet him before that we meet now?)

Alert:
You could play. (Past capacity + work done)
You could have played. (Past capacity + work not done)

Exercise
Change these sentences into negative and interrogative forms.

I could have taken money from him. They could have paid the bill. The child could have sung well. Your brother could have learnt music. The doctor could have cured the patient. The soldier could have saved their lives. We could have given him a chance.

Should have + V³

It describes that it was your duty to do the work that you did not do.

Hint: Past Duty + Work not done
Rule: Sub + should have + v3 + object

Affirmative

We should have told him the truth.
(It means: It was our duty to tell him the truth but we did not tell)
He should have left politics.
(It means: He was supposed to leave politics but he did not leave)
You should have married her.
(It means: You were supposed to marry her but you did not)
The negotiator should have understood the reality.
(It means: The negotiator was supposed to understand the reality but he did not)

Negative

They should not have rejected the proposal.
(It means: They were not supposed to reject the proposal but they rejected)
We should not have believed him.
(It means: We were not supposed to believe him but we did)
She should not have taken the medicine.
(It means: She was not supposed to take the medicine but she did)
You should not have consulted a lawyer.
(It means: You were not supposed to consult a lawyer but you did)

Interrogative

Should he have deposited the money?
(It means: Was he supposed to deposit money that he did not?)
Should the children not have played hockey?
(It means: Were the children not supposed to play cricket that they did?)
Why should he have visited America?
(It means: Why was he supposed to visit America that he did?)
Why should I have helped him?
(It means: Why was I supposed to help him that I did?)

Alert:

You could have played. (Past Capability + work not done)
You should have played. (Past Duty + work not done)
You were supposed to play. (Work expected + not done)

Exercise
Change these sentences into negative and interrogative forms.
The teacher should have taught us today. I should have given him the book. The army should have captured the land. You should have repaired the machine. They should have gone abroad. The business should have flourished. The people should have voted for him.

Would have + V³
It describes that you had already done the work that you did not do.

Hint: Past Possibility + Work not done
Rule: Sub + would have + v3 + object

Affirmative
> You would have played cricket.
> *(It means: It was possible that you had played cricket but you did not play)*
> He would have become a doctor.
> *(It means: It was possible that you had become a doctor but he did not become)*
> You would have married her.
> *(It means: It was possible that you had married her but you did not marry)*
> The company would have developed technologies.
> *(It means: It was possible that the company had developed technologies but it did not do so)*

Negative
> He would not have written a letter.
> *(It means: It was not possible that he had written a letter but he wrote)*
> The doctor would not have cured the patient.
> *(It means: It was not possible that the doctor had cured the patient but he cured)*
> She would not have taken the medicine.
> *(It means: It was not possible that she had taken the medicine but she took)*
> You would not have consulted a lawyer.
> *(It means: It was not possible that you had consulted a lawyer but you did)*

Interrogative
> Would he have done his work?
> *(It means: Was it possible that he had done his work which he did not do?)*
> Would the doctor have cured the patient?
> *(It means: Was it possible that the doctor had cured the patient whom he did not cure?)*
> Would she not have taken the medicine?
> *(It means: Was it not possible that she had taken the medicine that she already took?)*
> What would the people have done till now?
> *(It means: What was possible for the people to have done till now?)*

Alert:
You could have played. (Past Capability + work not done)
You should have played. (Past Duty + work not done)
You would have played. (Past Possibility + work not done)

Exercise
Change these sentences into negative and interrogative forms.

The farmer would have ploughed the field. The magician would have played the magic. The dancer would have danced on the floor. The princess would have married the man. The criminal would have shot the woman. The government would have lost the majority. The hunter would have killed the animal.

May have + V³

It describes that you have already done the work in past.

Hint: Past Possibility + Work already done
Rule: Sub + may have + v3 + object

Affirmative

She may have done the work.
(It means: It is possible that she has already done the work)
You may have married her.
His brother may have become a doctor.
The child may have reached home.
The teacher may have taught the students.

Negative

They may not have reached station.
(It means: It is not possible that they have already reached)
The carpenter may not have measured it.
The leader may not have guided the people properly.
The president may not have taken right decision.
Anita may not have talked to Velvet.

Interrogative

May he have complained to the police?
(It means: Is it possible that he has already complained?)
May the doctor have cured the patient?
Why may she have committed the crime?
What may they have thought today?
May the children have watched the movie?

Alert:

You may have taught. (Past Possibility + work already done)
You might have taught. (Past Less Possibility + work already done)
You will have taught. (Future Perfect Tense: You will finish teaching in future)
You could have taught. (Past Capability + work not done)
You should have taught. (Past Duty + work not done)
You would have taught. (Past Possibility + work not done)
You must have taught. (Present Surety + work already done)

Exercise
Change these sentences into negative and interrogative forms.

He may have known the truth. The accused may have accepted the crime. The judge may have sentenced him. The woman may have delivered a child. It may have rained. They may have entered the sanctum. The police may have fired on the crowd.

Have had to
It is used to show that you are bound to do the work.

Rule: Sub + have had to / have got to + v1 + object

Affirmative
> I have had to pay for this.
> *(It means: I am bound to pay for this)*
> I have got to pay for this.
> *(Same meaning: I am bound to pay for this)*
> You have had to go from here.
> She has had to repair her computer.
> They have had to have this medicine.

Negative
> We have not had to sit in the train.
> She has not had to marry you.
> They have not got to be patient.
> The people have not had to leave the place.
> She has not had to say anything.

Interrogative
> Have I had to diagnose the problem?
> Have you got to say anything?
> Why have I had to know this?
> What has she got to do now?
> Have you got to set him right?

Alert:
I have to go. (Present Compulsion)
I have had to go. (Bound with the work)
I have got to go. (Bound with the work)
I am supposed to go. (Expectation)
I would like to go. (Preference)
I had better gone. (Condition)

Exercise

Change these sentences into negative and interrogative forms.

I have had to tell you the truth. She has got to go now. We have had to format the computer. She has got to be smart. They have had to change the decision. You have had to sell this car. The students have had to answer these questions.

Had had to

It is used to show that you were bound to do the work but perhaps you did not do.

Rule: Sub + had had to / had got to + v1 + object

Affirmative

She had had to visit the place.
(It means: She was bound to visit the place which she did not visit)
She had got to visit the place.
(Same meaning: She was bound to visit the place which she did not visit)
We had had to go there today.
He had had to do this work.
You had got to talk to him.

Negative

She had not had to say anything.
She had not got to say anything.
We had not had to sit in the train.
They had not got to be patient.
The people had not got to leave the place.

Interrogative

Had you had to learn computer?
Had you got to learn computer?
Had you had to take revenge on him?
Had he had to marry this year?
What had she got to do there?

Alert:

She had to sing. (Past Compulsion)
She had had to sing. (Bound with the work in past)
She had got to sing. (Bound with the work in past)
She had been singing. (Past Perfect Continuous Tense)
She had sung. (Pas Perfect Tense)

Exercise

Change these sentences into negative and interrogative forms.

I have had to tell you the truth. She has got to go now. We have had to format the computer. She has got to be smart. They have had to change the decision. You have had to sell this car. The students have had to answer these questions.

Could have had to

This modal is used to describe that you could have done the work in compulsyon but you did not do.

Hint: Past Capability + Compulsion + Work not done
Rule: Sub + could have had to + v1 + object

Affirmative
>We could have had to go there.
>*(It means: We could have compulsorily gone there but we did not go)*
>She could have had to learn French.
>Her sister could have had to join army.
>You could have had to take this medicine.
>They could have had to accept defeat.

Negative
>The farmer could not have had to wait for rain.
>You could not have had to work so hard.
>The child could not have had to face so much of trouble.
>They could not have had to buy anything.
>The people could not have had to leave the place.

Interrogative
>Could we have had to talk to him?
>Could the police have had to arrest him?
>Could I have had to answer these questions?
>Why could they have had to go to the doctor?
>Why could you have had to set him free?

Alert:
I had to play. (Past Compulsion)
I had had to play. (Bound with the work in past)
I could have played. (Past Capability + work not done)
I could have had to play. (Past Capability + Compulsion + work not done)

Exercise

Change these sentences into negative and interrogative forms.

She could have had to accept her mistake. I could have had to help him. They could have had to learn programming. You could have had to work hard for the exam. The people could have had to join revolution. You could have had to know the fact. The teacher could have had to come to school early.

Would have had to
This modal is used to describe that you would have done the work in compulsion but you did not do.

Hint: Past possibility + Compulsion + work not done)
Rule: Sub + would have had to + v1 + object

Affirmative
>He would have had to drink coffee.
>*(It means: He would have compulsorily drunk coffee but he did not)*
>The teacher would have had to teach new lessons.
>The army would have had to kill the intruders.
>They would have had to call the police.
>The suspect would have had to admit the crime.
>The people would have had to leave politics.

Negative
>He would not have had to come here.
>The people would not have had to become so hostile.
>I would not have had to sit so long.
>They would not have had to read this book.
>He would not have had to write this letter.
>I would not have had to say anything.

Interrogative
>Would I have had to answer these questions?
>Would they have had to challenge the government?
>Why would they have had to go to the doctor?
>Why would you have had to set him free?
>Would we have had to talk to him?
>Would the police have had to arrest him?

Alert:
He would write. (Past Possibility)
He would have to write. (Past Possibility + Compulsion)
He would have written. (Past Possibility + work not done)
He would have had to write. (Past possibility + Compulsion + work not done)

Exercise

Change these sentences into negative and interrogative forms.

You would have had to know the fact. The teacher would have had to come to school early. She would have had to accept her mistake. I would have had to help him. They would have had to learn programming. You would have had to work hard for the exam. The people would have had to join revolution.

May have had to

This modal is used to describe that you may have done the work in compulsion.

Hint: Past possibility + Compulsion + <u>work already done</u>)
Rule: Sub + may have had to + v1 + object

Affirmative

He may have had to leave the work.
(It means: He may have compulsorily left the work)
They may have had to steal money.
She may have had to go America.
The manager may have had to deduct his salary.
The public may have had to support the system.

Negative

The teacher may not have had to buy books.
She may not have had to visit the beaches.
The tourist may not have had to book the ticket.
The company may not have had to hire the people.
The judge may not have had to ask any question.

Interrogative

May he have had to look for another job?
May she have had to find the proof?
May the doctor have had to inject the patient?
May the author have had to do a research?
May he have had to finish study in teenage?

Alert

You will have to sing. *(Future Compulsion)*
You would have to sing. *(Past Possibility + Compulsion)*
You may have to sing. *(Present Possibility + Compulsion)*
You should have to sing. *(Obligatory Compulsion)*
You must have to sing. *(Strong Compulsion)*
You have had to sing. *(You have got to sing).*
You had had to sing. *(You had got to sing).*
You are having to sing. *(You are singing in compulsive situation).*

You will have sung. *(Future Perfect Tense)*
You could have sung. *(Past Capacity + Work not done)*
You should have sung. *(Past Obligation + Work not done)*
You would have sung. *(Past Possibility + Work not done)*
You may have sung. *(Past Possibility + Work done)*
You must have sung. *(Present Perfect + Work done)*
You could have had to sing. *(Past Capacity + Compulsion + Work not done)*
You would have had to sing. *(Past Possibility + Compulsion + Work not done)*
You may have had to sing. *(Past Possibility + Compulsion + Work done)*

Active Passive Voice

Voice is the form of a verb that describes the relation of a subject to the action.

Present Indefinite

Affirmative

Active Voice
The sentence that represents the subject primarily is called Active Voice.
Sub + v1 / v5 + object
You play cricket.

Passive Voice
The sentence that represents the object primarily is called Passive Voice.
Object + is / am / are + v3 + by + sub
Cricket is played by you.

Bare Passive
The sentence that represents the object primarily without subject is called Bare Passive Voice.
Object + is / am / are + v3 + additional
Cricket is played here.

Negative

Active: Sub + do / does + not + v1 + object
I do not teach him.

Passive: Object + is / am / are + not + v3 + by + sub
He is not taught by me.

Bare Passive: Object + is / am / are + not + v3 + additional
He is not taught English.

Interrogative

Active: Do / does + sub + v1 + object
Does she watch films?

Passive: Is / am / are + object + v3 + by + sub
Are the films watched by her?

Bare Passive: Is / am / are + object + v3 + additional
Are these films watched?

Exercise
Change these sentences into passive voice only (not bare passive).

I play music. She plays football. They help me. You do not take coffee. She does not learn computer. The man does not speak Spanish. Do you sing songs? Do they not sell cars? What do you teach him? When does she study mathematics?

Present Continuous

Affirmative
Active: Sub + is / am / are + v4 + object
He is painting the walls.

Passive: Object + is / am / are + being + v3 + by + sub
The walls are being painted by him.

Bare Passive: Object + is / am / are + being + v3 + additional
The walls are being painted.

Negative
Active: She is not doing the work.
Passive: The work is not being done by her.
Bare Passive: The work is not being done today.

Interrogative
Active: Are you calling me?
Passive: Am I being called by you?
Bare Passive: Am I being called there?

Alert

I teach.	(It means: I do the work – Active)
I am taught.	(It means: The work is done upon me – Bare Passive)
I am teaching.	(It means: I am doing the work – Active)
I am being taught.	(It means: The work is being done upon me – Bare Passive)
What do you do here?	(Present Indefinite – Active)
What is done here?	(Present Indefinite – Bare Passive)
What are you doing here?	(Present Continuous – Active)
What is being done here?	(Present Continuous – Bare Passive)

Exercise

Change these sentences into passive voice only.

You earn money. You are earning money. She does not question you. She is not questioning you. Do we help poor? Are we helping poor? Why do the police beat him? Why are the police beating him? What do you do here? What are you doing here?

Present Perfect

Affirmative
Active: Sub + have / has + v3 + object
We have revealed the truth.

Passive: Object + has / have + been + v3 + by + sub
The truth has been revealed by us.

Bare Passive: Object + has / have + been + v3 + additional
The truth has been revealed today.

Negative
Active: They have not cheated him.
Passive: He has not been cheated by them.
Bare Passive: He has not been cheated.

Interrogative
Active: Have you understood the fact?
Passive: Has the fact been understood by you?
Bare Passive: Has the fact been understood?

Alert

You have given money.	(Active Voice)
You have been given money.	(Bare Passive Voice)
You have been giving money.	(Present Perfect Continuous Tense)
You have to give money.	(Modal Verb of Compulsion)

Exercise

Change these sentences into passive voice only.

Does she solve problems? Is she solving problems? Has she solved problems? What does the teacher ask them? What is the teacher asking them? What has the teacher asked them? How do you spend money? How are you spending money? How have you spent money? What do you play there? What are you playing there? What have you played there? Does he not speak English? Is he not speaking English? Has he not spoken English?

Past Indefinite

Affirmative
Active: Sub + v2 + object – He killed the tiger.
Passive: Object + was / were + v3 + by + sub – The tiger was killed by him.
Bare Passive: Object + was / were + v3 + additional – The tiger was killed.

Negative
Active: I did not forgive him.
Passive: He was not forgiven by me.
Bare Passive: He was not forgiven.

Interrogative
Active: What did you advise them?
Passive: What were they advised by you?
Bare Passive: What were they advised?

Past Continuous

Affirmative
Active: Sub + was / were + v4 + object – He was scolding the children.
Passive: Object + was / were + being + v3 + by + sub – The children were being scolded by him.
Bare Passive: Object + was / were + being + v3 + additional – The children were being scolded there.

Negative
Active: They were not encouraging the people.
Passive: The people were not being encouraged by them.
Bare Passive: The people were not being encouraged.

Interrogative
Active: Was she not cooking food?
Passive: Was the food not being cooked by her?
Bare Passive: Was the food not being cooked there?

Alert

He appreciated the work.	(Past Indefinite – Active Voice)
He was appreciated for the work.	(Past Indefinite – Bare Passive)
He has been appreciated for the work.	(Present Perfect – Bare Passive)
You did not support.	(Past Indefinite – Active Voice)
You were not supported.	(Past Indefinite – Bare Passive)
You wee not supporting.	(Past Continuous – Active Voice)
You were not being supported.	(Past Continuous – Bare Passive Voice)

Exercise
Change these sentences into passive voice only.

Do you call her? Are you calling her? Have you called her? Did you call her? Were you calling her? How does she help them? How is she helping them? How has she helped them? How did she help them? How was she helping them?

Past Perfect

Affirmative
Active: Sub + had + v3 + object – They had won the match.
Passive: Object + had + been + v3 + by + sub – The match had been won by them.
Bare Passive: Object + had + been + v3 + additional – The match had been won.

Negative
Active: She had not told anything.
Passive: Nothing had been told by her.
Bare Passive: Nothing had been told yet.

Interrogative
Active: Had you completed the work?
Passive: Had the work been completed by you?
Bare Passive: Had the work been completed?

Future Indefinite

Affirmative
Active: Sub + will + v1 + object – He will send the children to school.
Passive: Object +will be + v3 + by + sub – The children will be sent to school by him.
Bare Passive: Object + will be + v3 + additional – The children will be sent to school today.

Negative
Active: They will not accept defeat.
Passive: The defeat will not be accepted by them.
Bare Passive: The defeat will not be accepted.

Interrogative
Active: How will you solve this problem?
Passive: How will this problem be solved by you?
Bare Passive: How will this problem be solved?

Alert

He had punished.	(Active Voice)
He had been punished.	(Bare Passive Voice)
He had been punishing.	(Past Perfect Continuous Tense)
He had to punish.	(Modal Verb of Past Compulsion)
You will bless.	(Active Voice)
You will be blessed.	(Bare Passive Voice)
You will be blessing.	(Future Continuous Tense)

Exercise
Change these sentences into passive voice only.
I buy books. I am buying books. I have bought books. I bought books. I was buying books. I had bought books. I will buy books. She helps me. She is helping me. She has helped me. She helped me. She was helping me. She had helped me. She will help me.

Future Perfect

Affirmative
Active: Sub + will have + v3 + object – He will have played the trick.
Passive: Object + will have + been + v3 + by + sub – The trick will have been played by him.
Bare Passive: Object + will have + been + v3 + additional – The trick will have been played by then.

Negative
Active: They will not have broken the promise.
Passive: The promise will not have been broken by them.
Bare Passive: The promise will not have been broken.

Interrogative
Active: Will you have found the destination?
Passive: Will the destination have been found by you?
Bare Passive: Will the destination have been found?

Alert

I will inform.	(Active Voice)
I will be informed.	(Bare Passive Voice)
I will have informed.	(Active Voice)
I will have been informed.	(Bare Passive Voice)

Exercise
Change these sentences into passive voice only.
I drink coffee. I am drinking coffee. I have drunk coffee. I drank coffee. I was drinking coffee. I had drunk coffee. I will drink coffee. I will have drunk coffee. What do you ask him? What are you asking him? What have you asked him? What did you ask him? What were you asking him? What had you asked him? What will you ask him? What will you have asked him?

Exercise
Change these sentences into passive voice only.

I teach you. I am teaching you. I have taught you. I taught you. I was teaching you. I had taught you. Why does she take medicine? Why is she taking medicine? Why has she taken medicine? Why did she take medicine? Why was she taking medicine? Why had she taken medicine? Does the child narrate stories? Is the child narrating stories? Has the child narrated stories? Did the child narrate stories? Did you see him? Does he run a business? Why was he writing a letter? How did you lose that? When did the people start revolution? She is cheating you. They have defeated the enemy. How did you recognize him? How will I forget him? When will you do this work? Did she return the book? Did you not diagnose the problem? Do you appreciate his work? Will they punish the terrorist? Has she published the news? When did you remove the luggage? We speak English. We are speaking English. We have spoken English. We spoke English. We were speaking English. We had spoken English. We will speak English. We will have spoken English.

Voice of Modals
Can / Could/ Should / Would / May / Might / Must

Affirmative
Active: Sub + modal + v1 + object
You should do this work.

Passive: Object + modal + be + v3 + by + sub
This work should be done by you.

Bare Passive: Object + modal + be + v3 + additional
This work should be done today.

Continuous: Sub + modal + be +v4 + object
You should be doing this work.

Negative
Active: He would not teach German.
Passive: German would not be taught by him.
Bare Passive: German would not be taught in class.
Continuous: He would not be teaching German.

Interrogative
Active: Why can they not answer the questions?
Passive: Why can the questions not be answered by them?
Bare Passive: Why can the questions not be answered?

Have to / Has to / Had to

Affirmative
Active: Sub + modal + v1 + object
She has to drive this car.

Passive: Object + modal + be + v3 + by + sub
This car has to be driven by her.

Bare Passive: Object + modal + be + v3 + additional
This car has to be driven.

Continuous: Sub + modal + be +v4 + object
She has to be driving this car.

Negative
Active: He had not to inform the police.
Passive: The police had not to be informed by him.
Bare Passive: The police had not to be informed for this matter.

Interrogative
Active: What have you to learn now?
Passive: What has to be learnt by you now?
Bare Passive: What has to be learnt now?

Could have / Should have / Would have / May have / Must have

Affirmative
Active: Sub + modal + v3 + object
I would have taught him.

Passive: Object + modal + been + v3 + by + sub
He would have been taught by me.

Bare Passive: Object + modal + been + v3 + additional
He would have been taught.

Continuous: Sub + modal + been +v4 + object
I would have been teaching him.

Negative
Active: They should not have praised him.
Passive: He should not have been praised by them.
Bare Passive: He should not have been praised.
Continuous: They should not have been praising him.

Interrogative
Active: Would she have written poems?
Passive: Would the poems have been written by her?
Bare Passive: Would these poems have been written?
Continuous: Would she have been writing poems?

Exercise
Change these sentences into passive voice only.

Can you drive this car? Could you drive this car? Should you drive this car? Would you drive this car? Have you to drive this car? Had you to drive this car? Could you have driven this car? Should you have driven this car? Would you have driven this car? May you have driven this car?

Smart Verbs

The verb which has many meanings is called Smart Verbs.

Have

Meaning 1: To possess something
I have a computer at my home.

Meaning 2: To eat or drink
Will you have a cup of coffee with me?

Meaning 3: To take
Have your seat please.
You guys have fun!

Meaning 4: To describe compulsion
She has to get this information from you.

Meaning 5: To get something done
When will you have your hair colored?
I will have him call you.

Would

Meaning 1: To show possibility of past
The teacher would teach you Spanish.

Meaning 2: To show less possibility in <u>present</u>
She would come here. (It means: There is a very less possibility of her to come)

Meaning 3: To describe irregular repeated action of past
His father would give him money. (It means: His father gave money on irregular schedule of time)
His father used to give him money. (It means: His father gave money on regular schedule of time)

Meaning 4: To show request
Would you tell me you email address?

Meaning 5: To wish
Would that he was here! (It means: You wish he should be here)

Meaning 6: In indirect narration, will is replaced with would
I said, "I will play."
I said that I would play.

Get

Meaning 1: To achieve
How much did you get for it?

Meaning 2: To feel
I am getting cold.

Meaning 3: To understand
She got your point very clearly.

Meaning 4: To make something available
Get me your manager on the phone.

Meaning 5: To get a work done
They will get this work done today.

Meaning 6: To happen
It is getting darker now.

Go

Meaning 1: To proceed
When is he going from here?

Meaning 2: To become
Why are you going mad about it?

Meaning 3: To be sold
How are the mangoes going these days? (It means: What is the price of mangoes?)

Meaning 4: Success (Noun)
This is a big go of my life.

Meaning 5: Progressive
I am go. (It means: I am progressive)

Alert

You have to play.	(Present Compulsion)
You are having to play.	(Continuous Compulsion)
You are to have played.	(You are in the condition to have finished playing)
You have had to play.	(You have got the urgency to play)
You have to have him play.	(You have to make him play)
You have to have dinner.	(You have to eat)
You have to have your sister married.	(You have to do the arrangement for your sister's marriage)
She would go to school.	(Perhaps she went to school in past)
She would go to school.	(She used to go to school)
She would go to school.	(She will go to school but there is vey less possibility)
She might go to school.	(There is vey less possibility that she will go to school)

Look

Meaning 1: To put eyes at a direction
Look at the girls dancing there.

Meaning 2: To appear
You look very tired today.

Meaning 3: Fashion (Noun)
Go for the originality, not only the look.

Meaning 4: Appearance (Noun)
The look of this hotel has to be changed.

Meaning 5: The way when you look at something (Noun)
She gave me a look from the corner.

Do

Meaning 1: To do any work
When are you doing your homework?

Meaning 2: To study
I did English in my school.

Meaning 3: To solve
He did the puzzle in a second.

Meaning 4: To be suitable
It will not do for me.

Meaning 5: To stress on what you say
I do know him very well. (It means: I am sure that I know him)

May

Meaning 1: Possibility
She may pass this exam.

Meaning 2: Order / Request
You may leave now.
May I have your address please?

Meaning 3: Wish
May you get the victory!

Meaning 4: Might = very less possibility
They might accept my proposal.

Meaning 5: Might = Power (Noun)
Truth disappears in the shadow of might.

Be
Meaning 1: is, am, are, was, were
I am to leave from here now.

Meaning 2: To become
Will you be my friend?

Meaning 3: To be
You have to be positive about it.

Meaning 4: To order something to happen
The judge said, "He be hanged. "
Praised to be Jesus Christ!

Meaning 5: Being = existence
They are losing their being.

Make
Meaning 1: To prepare something
Are you making your breakfast?

Meaning 2: To earn money
What business are they making money from?

Meaning 3: To do
You have to make it fast.
Don't make haste.

Meaning 4: To compel someone
Don't make me slap you.

Meaning 5: To set
Two and two makes four.

Meaning 6: To make something pleasant
God bless you, you made my day! (You made me happy)

Keep
Meaning 1: To continue
I kept on moving ahead.

Meaning 2: To keep something to sell
Do you keep pens?

Meaning 3: To hold someone from doing something
You can't keep me informing the police.
What kept you there so long?

Meaning 4: To maintain
He is not keeping well today.

Meaning 5: Illegal wife (Noun)
Does he have a keep with him?

Happen
Meaning 1: To occur
What is happening there?

Meaning 2: To get a chance
If I happen to meet, what should I ask him?

Meaning 3: Perhaps
Happen, he may be late.

Meaning 4: Happening = exciting
He has a very happening career ahead.

Infinitive to
I am to teach him.
(It mean: I am about to teach him)

Were you to buy this book?
(It mean: Were you about to buy this book?)

What are they to do now?
(It mean: What are they about to do now?)

He looks to have lost.
(It mean: It appears that he has been lost)

I am sorry to have left you.
(It mean: I am sorry that I could not reach or find you)

They are to be punished.
(It mean: Bare Passive Voice = They are about to get punishment)

See
To look at
I saw a picture hanging at the wall.

To meet
She will see me next week.

To understand
We see that nothing can happen now.

Let = allow
Let him go.
Let it be done.
Would you let me know this?
Let me tell you something about it.
Let us say that, what would you do if they don't come here?

Going to
I am going to meet him.
She is going to come today.
They are going to be rich.
It is going to happen.
We are going to go.

There
What are you doing there? (Place)
There was a king. (In that matter)
There you are! (I found you or your point)

It
I found it. (The thing)
It is raining here. (Standby 'It')
It (the animal) is so cute. (It is used when the sex of the animal is unknown)

Take
Take heart. (Be courageous)
It took five minutes to reach here.
Take it easy.
Take me to the forest. (Reach me)
Take it from me. (Believe me)

Come
Come to the point.
Please come again. (Repeat what you said)
The dream is coming true. (Happening true)
She is giving me a come-on. (Encouraging me for love)

Preposition

It is a word used before a noun or pronoun to relate it to another word or the part of a sentence.

About

1. for time

It is about four o'clock.

2. to be ready

He is about to leave.

3. the subject matter

What are you talking about?

4. planning

I know what she is about.

Above

1. over

The fan is hanging above the table.

2. more than

You are getting above your salary.

3. more rich

He married in above his family.

4. senior

The clerk should respect his above.

5. not to be understood

French is above you.

6. higher or wiser

You speak above your age.

After

1. late in time

Don't read after midnight.

2. planning to get

The pick-pocket is after his money.

3. because of

He died after malaria.

4. above from

Give me all you have after four hundred Rs.

5. behind

I am after you.

6. later in the age

He changed his career after twenty-five.

7. on the name of

He was named after the name of the city.

Exercise: *Fill in the blanks with correct preposition.*

Buying this property is – your reach. He is – to come here in a minute. What are they – to do now? This testimony is – the truth. When he speaks, he sounds – bravery. Is it what are you – to plan? His performance is – average. You can not prove yourself – your knowledge. The thief is – his watch. I guess it broke – I left for office.

At
1. to show time
The bus reached me at ten pm.
2. to mention place
He is standing at the gate.
3. near
The temple is at the river.
4. according to
He was hired at hundred Rs. a day.
5. direction
What are you looking at?
6. the place
He will live rest of his life at village.
7. for the speed
The car is running at full speed.
8. turn of time
She agreed to marry me at last.
9. the state
The old man is at death.
10. condition
Getting furious at what I saw, I slapped him.

Against
1. unwilling
The public is against the vote.
2. opposite
I was standing against the tree.
3. for
He received five thousand Rs. against the rent.
4. unfavorable
The boat is sailing against the wind.

Before
1. earlier the time
There was no one before two pm.
2. in front of
Everything is open before you.
3. old time
Education was not so important before.

Exercise: *Fill in the blanks with correct preposition.*
Nothing is hidden – you. He was given the loan – his property. She became a doctor – the age of forty.
They are looking – you through the window. The child started crying – you shouted to him. This work is –
to be completed. The revolutionaries are – the government.

By
1. by the means of
Are you going to market by car?
2. from the work of
This work can not be done by the labors.
3. with
The police caught the thief by his hair.
4. till
He will come back by evening.
5. for a measurement
The bullet missed him by an inch.
6. by the side of
He drove the car by the jungle.
7. beside
Come and sit by me.
8. according to
You will be paid by the week.

Behind
1. back
Who was standing behind the gate?
2. hidden
The police know the culprit behind the plot.
3. inferior than
I am not behind you.
4. back in the time
The watch is running behind the time.

From
1. for source
What do you want from me?
2. to mention the starting time
The school would open from 16th June.
3. to mention the place
How long the station is from here?
4. for the reason of
He died from fever.
5. belonging to
He is from a noble family.

Exercise: *Fill in the blanks with correct preposition.*

He looks ill – his face. His parents were – Japan. She will reach here – tomorrow. Pay him – the meter. Could you find anyone – this conspiracy? I rode the motorbike – the town. The old-man died – his native place. You can not hide your face – the crowd. The ladder was placed – the wall.

For
1. for the reason of
You have to pay for your deeds.
2. for the price of
I bought it for 10 Rs.
3. from the time
I have been waiting for two hours.
4. because of
He can die for his words.
5. because
For he traveled across the country, he got a lot of knowledge.
6. according to
This car runs 60 km for a liter.
7. the purpose
He ran for life.

In
1. in the place of
He is in London for three weeks.
2. in the time of
What were you doing in the morning?
3. in a period
I will meet you in a week.
4. inside
She is taking me in.
5. in color
Don't write in red.
6. on
The birds are sitting in the tree.
7. in the bed
The child is sleeping in the bed.

Into
1. inside
Look into the book.
2. deep down
He fell into the well.
3. late in the time
I saw her studying into the night.

Exercise: *Fill in the blanks with correct preposition.*

She sold the car – eighty thousand. What is there to see – Mumbai? Don't fall – this trap. I will see you – the morning. He took risk – his career. She looks to be – a decent family. If you look – it, you will find the difference. The game is – to start. Don't throw the ball – his head. He is running – money.

On
1. on something
Put the computer on the table.
2. on the day
I will be leaving on Tuesday.
3. to show the state
The officers are on the way for office.
4. on a period of
She is on maternity leave.
5. on the side of
He turned his back on the crowd.
6. continued
The war was on for the next two years.

Of
1. from
Beware of dogs!
2. made of
The jacket is made of leather.
3. of the country or place
The people of west neglect marriage.
4. out of
Which of you can run faster?
5. because of
She died of AIDS.

Off
1. away
Get off.
2. to the other side
Why is he sailing off the shore?
3. far
You have to go a little off Link Road.
4. the day when you don't work in office
I will have off next Monday.
5. dead
He is off.
6. do something to get away from it
I paid him off.

Exercise: *Fill in the blanks with correct preposition.*

They are going to start the work – Tuesday. One – them must be a thief. Place the monitor – the desk. This sweater is made – wool. Who is going to support you – this? Are you going to take me – the chamber? She is waiting – a long period of time. The school is going to start – June. No one is standing – the curtain.

Over
1. above
There is a clock hanging over his head.
2. from one side to another
The thief jumped over the wall.
3. more than
The car is running over 60.
4. end
The show is getting over.

To
1. to the place
He is going to America.
2. limited to
Keep it to yourself.
3. by
You are known to all.
4. infinitive to, to do something
I told him to talk to you.
5. in
Welcome to India.
6. near
Come to me before 6 pm.
7. till
Count from 10 to 25.
8. with
Multiply 4 to 6.
9. less in time
It is quarter to ten.
10. in
Don't take it to your heart.

Up
1. above
He was lifted up the hills.
2. ready to use
The internet is up now.
3. rise
The business is full of ups and downs.

Exercise: *Fill in the blanks with correct preposition.*

The horse jumped – the fence. She climbed – the hills. Go – him and take what he gives you. The airplane crossed – the tower. The traffic is moving smoothly – one side. He is trying to get up – the bed. What are you looking – the box? We should be patient when we are – trouble. Think again – you jump to a conclusion.

With
1. together with
He is living with his aunt.
2. with the help of
I am writing with a blue pen.
3. associated with
Start the work with proper plans.
4. in
His brain is washed with fanaticism.
5. of
The girl with sharp feature is my neighbor.

Some more prepositions

According to
Agreeably to
Along with
Away from
Because of
By dint of
By means of
By reason of
By virtue of
By way of
Conformably to
For the sake of
In accordance with
With reference to
In addition to
On the behalf of
In case of
In comparison to
In compliance with
In consequence of
In course of
In favor of
In lieu of

In order to
In reference to
In regard to
In the event of
On account of
On condition that
Owing to
With a view to

Exercise: *Fill in the blanks with correct preposition.*

He thinks – his age. We should diagnose the problem – resolve it. He is studying – passing the exam. She will be there – her boss. I got a call – Australia yesterday. They are struggling – the best result. You need to look – the computer screen. She has to find a job – her living. He reached there – the city was deserted.

Conjunction

A word that connects two words or two clauses is called conjunction.

Will you wait <u>until</u> I return?

You will pass the exam <u>if</u> you work hard.

Go slow <u>lest</u> you should fall.

Give him all the information <u>provided</u> you know the company's policy.

<u>Since</u> you say so, I must believe it.

Tell them <u>that</u> I will come.

He finished first <u>though</u> he began late.

She will not pay <u>unless</u> she is compelled.

<u>When</u> I was young, I thought so.

I don't know <u>when</u> he comes.

He found his watch <u>where</u> he had left it.

I don't understand <u>how</u> it all happened.

Make hay <u>while</u> the sun shines.

I know <u>why</u> he left us.

She should be honest <u>only then</u> she can become great.

They know <u>what</u> they should not speak.

Exercise: *Fill in the blanks with correct conjunction.*

You will not succeed – you work hard. Catch me – you can. I will stay – you return. Bread – milk is wholesome food. You will get the prize – you deserve it. I will be ruined – you do that. She is – tall – fair. Do you know – were you born? Try to understand the lesson – the teacher is teaching. I asked him – he was leaving for London.

I asked him <u>if</u> he was learning French.

<u>Either</u> take it <u>or</u> leave it.

It is <u>neither</u> useful <u>nor</u> ornamental.

We both love <u>and</u> honor him.

I waited <u>till</u> the train arrived.

He is richer <u>than</u> I am.

I did not come <u>because</u> you did not call me.

We arrived <u>after</u> you had gone.

Don't go <u>before</u> I come.

I was wandering <u>whether</u> you can help me.

Is the story true <u>or</u> false?

<u>Though</u> he is suffering pain, <u>yet</u> he does not complain.

<u>Not only</u> is he foolish, <u>but</u> obstinate also.

The notice was published <u>in order that</u> all might know the fact.

I will forgive you <u>on the condition that</u> you do not repeat it.

Such an act would not be kind <u>even if</u> you were just.

He saved some bread <u>so that</u> he should not go hungry.

He walks <u>as though</u> he is slightly lame.

I must refuse your request, <u>in as much as</u> I believe it unreasonable.

Exercise: *fill in the blanks with correct conjunction.*

He is not strong – he is gone to fight. You call me – you reach there. She behaves – she is innocent. I was late – I had no watch. He should not be so cruel – he is illiterate. You – your friend must have done it. She called me – I should help her with money. He thinks he is smarter – everyone. Teach her home – send her to school.

Five years have passed <u>since</u> he began to work.
She must weep <u>or</u> she will die.
A boy <u>who</u> tells lies gets punished.
He <u>as well as</u> his friend was present there.
He took off his coat <u>as soon as</u> he entered the house.
You look <u>as if</u> you are tired.
He is slow <u>but</u> he is sure.
I was annoyed, <u>still</u> I kept quiet.
I would come <u>only that</u> I am engaged.
They do not move <u>nor</u> do they spin.
Walk quickly; <u>else</u> you will not overtake him.
Something certainly fell in, <u>for</u> I heard a splash.
A famous book, <u>though</u>, there is nothing in it.
<u>As</u> he was not there, I spoke to his brother.
<u>Except</u> you repent, you can not do anything else.
Many things have happened <u>since</u> I saw you.
If I am blunt, <u>yet</u> I am honest.
I wonder <u>if</u> he will come.
<u>Not that</u> I loved her less <u>but that</u> I loved her family more.
He kept quiet <u>that</u> the dispute might cease.
The girls sang <u>while</u> the boys played.
The day is pleasant <u>only rather</u> cold.
So rich is he <u>that</u> he can buy a car.
It is because he is weak <u>that</u> he can not run.
<u>Since that</u> it is raining, we should not go out.
<u>Even if</u> you abuse me, I will continue to love you.
It seems <u>as if / as though</u> it would rain.
<u>No sooner</u> I cam in he asked me the question.
I know <u>that</u> is why I do not boast.
However poor he may be <u>but</u> he is happy.

Exercise: *fill in the blanks with correct conjunction.*

Give me to drink — I will die of thirst. He deserved to succeed — he worked hard. He will be sure to come — you invite him. We can travel by land or water. The earth is larger — the moon. Either you are mistaken — I am. I hear that your brother is in America. Be just — do not fear. I am sure — he said so. I ran fast — I missed the train.

Direct Indirect Narration

Direct: Steve said, "I speak French."
Indirect: Steve said that he spoke French.

Steve said to me, "You do not speak French."
Steve told me that I did not speak French.

I said to Steve, "I speak German."
I told Steve that I spoke German.

Steve said to Sophia, "Do you speak German?"
Steve asked Sophia if she spoke German.

I said to Sophia, "What does Steve speak?"
I asked Sophia what Steve spoke.

Sophia said to Steve, "Where are you going?"
Sophia asked Steve where he was going.

I said to Sophia, "How do you know Steve?"
I asked Sophia how she knew Steve.

Sophia said to me, "Steve is my friend."
Sophia told me that Steve was her friend.

Sophia said to Joseph, "What were you doing in the afternoon?"
Sophia asked Joseph what he was doing in the afternoon.

Joseph said to me, "I was watching a movie."
Joseph told me that he was watching a movie.

I said to Joseph, "Which movie did you watch?"
I asked Joseph which movie he had watched.

Joseph said, "It was an English movie."
Joseph said that that was an English movie.

Exercise: *Change these sentences into indirect narration.*

She said to me, "Do you play cricket?" I said to her, "I do not play cricket." She said to me, "Where are you going?" I said to her, "I am going to school." I said to Joseph, "Is she not going to school?" Joseph said to me, "She is going to market now." She said to Joseph, "My friend is calling me."

The changing words:
today – that day
yesterday – previous day
this – that
ago – before

tomorrow – next day
here – there
now – then
thus – so

I said to Sophia, "Who had given him money?"
I asked Sophia who had given him money.

Joseph said to me, "My father had given me money."
Joseph told me that his father had given him money.

Steve said to Joseph, "You have been very smart."
Steve told Joseph that he had been very smart.

I said to Suzan, "Will you buy the book today?"
I asked Suzan if she would buy the book that day.

Suzan said to me, "Can you do me a favor?"
Suzan asked me if I could do her a favor.

Sophia said to me, "I have to tell you something."
Sophia told me that she had to tell me something.

I said to my boss, "Shall I take a leave?"
I asked my boss if I should take a leave.

The teacher said to me, "You may have to learn Spanish."
The teacher told me that I might have to learn Spanish.

I said to Suzan, "You could have passed the exam."
I told Suzan that she could have passed the exam.

He said, "Let us wait for the award."
He proposed that they should wait for the award.

They said, "Yes, we can do this work."
They affirmed that they can do that work.

I said to Joseph, "Give me a glass of water."
I asked / requested Joseph to give me a glass of water.

My boss said, "Bring me the car."
My boss ordered me to bring him the car.

Exercise: *Change these sentences into indirect narration.*
I said to Suzan, "What are you doing today?" Suzan said to me, "I am going to play football." I said to her, "Is Steve also playing with you?" She said to me, "He does not like football." Steve said to me, "I play cricket only." I said to Steve, "I played cricket before."

Joseph said to Steve, "Don't touch the box."
Joseph forbade Steve from touching the box. Or, Joseph told Steve not to touch the box.

I said, "What a nice idea!"
I exclaimed with joy and said that was a nice idea.

Steve said to me, "Happy Christmas!"
Steve wished me a happy Christmas.

I said, "God is the protector of all."
I said that God is the protector of all.

She said, "It may rain today."
She guessed the possibility of rain that day.

I said, "What a pity!"
I regretted and said that was pitiful.

I said to him, "May you live long!"
I wished him a long life.

He said to the children, "Work hard if you want success."
He told the children to work hard if they wanted success.

The patient said, "Is the doctor about to leave?"
The patient enquired if the doctor was about to leave.

He said, "I don't have my involvement in this case."
He denied his involvement in that case.

I said to my friends, "Let us go."
I told my friends that we should go.

The teacher said, "I shall explain this to you."
The teacher said that he would explain that to them.

The judge said, "Call the first witness."
The judge commanded them to call the first witness.

He shouted, "Let me go."
He shouted to them to let him go.

Exercise: *change these sentences into indirect narration.*

The teacher said to the students, "Don't make a noise." I said to my friend, "What a nice joke!" My father said to me, "Give me a glass of water." The commander said to the army, "Fire." They said, "The Tajmahal is the beauty of India." My friend said to me, "Happy new year!" The man said to the conductor, "I don't have any change."

He said, "Be quiet and listen to my words."
He urged them to be quiet and listen to his words.

He said, "Alas! I am undone."
He exclaimed sadly that he was undone.

She said, "How clever I am!"
She said that she was very clever.

He said, "Bravo! You have done well."
He applauded him saying that he had done well.

"Run away, children," said their mother.
The mother told the children to run away.

"Hurry up," he said to his servant, "do not waste time."
He told his servant to hurry up and not waste time.

"What a stupid fellow you are!" he angrily remarked.
He said that he was very stupid.

"Halt!" shouted the officer to his men.
The officer shouted to his men and said to halt.

The poor man exclaimed, "Will none of you help me?"
The poor man asked if none of them would help him.

"Don't you know the way home?" asked I.
I asked if he did not know the way home.

Then aloud he said, "Tell me, boy, is the woman within?"
He asked the boy if the woman was within.

Exercise: *Change these sentences into indirect narration.*

"My son," said he, "a great treasure lies hidden in the estate I am about to leave you." "Where is it hidden?" said the sons. "I am about to leave you." said the old man, "but you must dig for it." "We will do that," said the sons to their father.

Some Verb-forms

Write	wrote	written
Speak	spoke	spoken
Read	read	read
Teach	taught	taught
Run	ran	run
Take	took	taken
Give	gave	given
Buy	bought	bought
Sell	sold	sold
Cry	cried	cried
Laugh	laughed	laughed
Beat	beat	beaten
Scold	scolded	scolded
Tell	told	told
Send	sent	sent
Hear	heard	heard
Win	won	won
Do	did	done
Narrate	narrated	narrated
Love	loved	loved
Sing	sang	sung
Abuse	abused	abused
Get	got	gotten / got
Live	lived	lived
Help	helped	helped
Ask	asked	asked
Answer	answered	answered
Like	liked	liked
Trust	trusted	trusted
Stay	stayed	stayed
Play	played	played
See	saw	seen
Drink	drank	drunk
Eat	ate	eaten
Go	went	gone
Come	came	come
Cheat	cheated	cheated
Make	made	made
Kill	killed	killed
Die	died	died
Defeat	defeated	defeated
Advise	advised	advised
Break	broke	broken
Marry	married	married
Drive	drove	driven
Call	called	called

Reach	reached	reached
Put	put	put
Show	showed	showed
Sit	sat	sat
Talk	talked	talked
Meet	met	met
Know	knew	known
Arrest	arrested	arrested
Understand	understood	understood
Learn	learnt	learnt
Fight	fought	fought
Forget	forgot	forgotten

Thank you for learning this much!
Now with this knowledge, you can do everything in English.
If you need to learn more, please refer to my next book DYNAMIC GRAMMAR OF ENGLISH

Niranjan Jha Showman
Trainer, Author, Physician, Entrepreneur, Filmmaker, Activist
Founder of Cromosys Corporation
facebook.com/cromosys
+91-9561450045
cromosys@yahoo.com
Nallasopara (W), Mumbai, India

Communicate with People

Listen to Them Carefully

Engage in Conversation

Develop Your Style

Read As Much As Possible

Speak Confidently

NIRANJAN JHA SHOWMAN

Founder - Niranjan Jha Showman

Education and Technology Research Center

Patankar Park, Nallasopara (W), Mumbai. +91-9561450045

Education, Technology, Publication, Healthcare, Newsmedia, Realtor, Filmmaking

www.facebook.com/cromosys

Cromosys Publication
Teach
Yourself
German
NIRANJAN JHA SHOWMAN

Cromosys Publication
Teach
Yourself
French
NIRANJAN JHA SHOWMAN

Cromosys Publication
Teach
Yourself
Spanish
NIRANJAN JHA SHOWMAN

Cromosys Publication

English
Voice
Accent and
Pronunciation

NIRANJAN JHA SHOWMAN

Teach Yourself Autodesk MAYA

Cromosys Publication

NIRANJAN JHA SHOWMAN

Cromosys Publication
Teach
Yourself
Autodesk
3ds Max
NIRANJAN JHA SHOWMAN

Cromosys Publication
CRIMINAL FACTORY
NIRANJAN JHA SHOWMAN

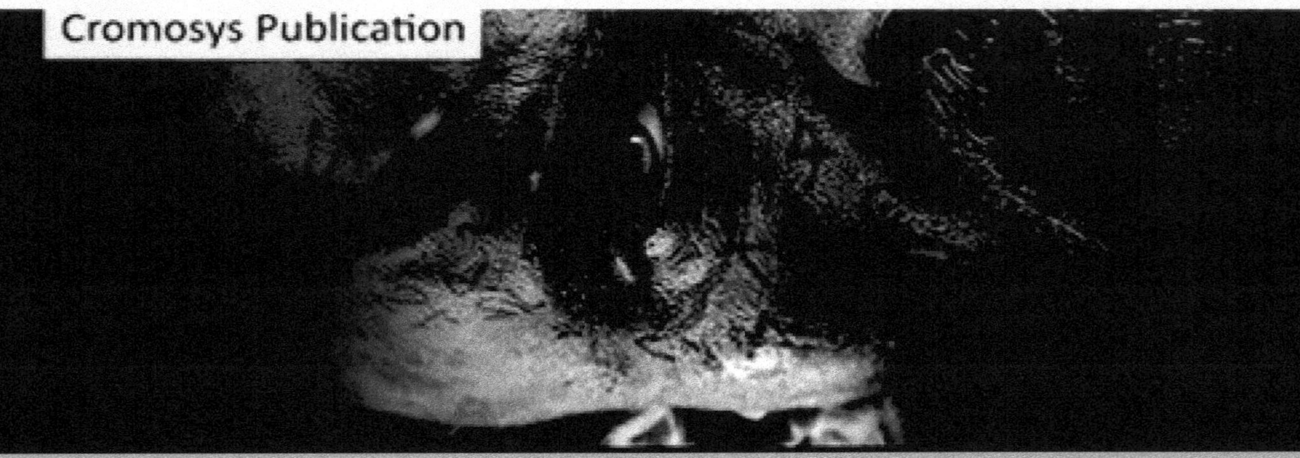

NIRANJAN JHA SHOWMAN
FOCAL DISASTER
Cromosys Publication

Cromosys Publication
Your talents will not help you succeed without your skill of using them.
NIRANJAN JHA SHOWMAN
BE
MILLIONAIRE
LIKE
ME

Extracts
from the Register
of Copyrights

Dated : 22/07/2022

1.	Registration Number	: **N-86788/2022**
2.	Name, address and nationality of the applicant	: **NIRANJAN JHA SHOWMAN, CROMOSYS PUBLICATION, 001, JAYSATYAM, PATANKAR ROAD, NALLASOPARA (W), MUMBAI, MAHARASHTRA - 401203. INDIAN**
3.	Nature of the applicant's interest in the copyright of the work	: **AUTHOR**
4.	Class and description of the work	: **LITERARY / BOOK**
5.	Title of the work	: **ENGLISH SPEAKING AND GRAMMAR**
6.	Language of the work	: **ENGLISH**
7.	Name, address and nationality of the author and if the author is deceased, date of his decease	: **NIRANJAN JHA SHOWMAN, CROMOSYS PUBLICATION, 001, JAYSATYAM, PATANKAR ROAD, NALLASOPARA (W), MUMBAI, MAHARASHTRA - 401203. INDIAN**
8.	Whether the work is published or unpublished	: **UNPUBLISHED**
9.	Year and country of first publication and name, address and nationality of the publisher	: **N.A.**
10.	Years and countries of subsequent publications, if any, and names, addresses and nationalities of the publishers	: **N.A.** **SAME AS ABOVE**
11.	Names, addresses and nationalities of the owners of various rights comprising the copyright in the work and the extent of rights held by each, together with particulars of assignments and licences, if any	:
12.	Names, addresses and nationalities of other persons, if any, authorised to assign or licence of rights comprising the copyright	: **N.A.**
13.	If the work is an 'Artistic work', the location of the original work, including name, address and nationality of the person in possession of the work. (In the case of an architectural work, the year of completion of the work should also be shown).	: **N.A.**
14.	If the work is an 'Artistic work', whether it is registered under the Designs Act 2000 if yes give details.	: **N.A.**
15.	If the work is an 'Artistic work', capable of being registered as a design under the Designs Act 2000.whether it has been applied to an article though an industrial process and ,if yes ,the number of times it is reproduced.	: **N.A.**
16.	Remarks, if any	:

Diary Number :	5395/2020-CO/N
Date of Application :	05/05/2020
Date of Receipt :	05/05/2020

DEPUTY REGISTRAR OF COPYRIGHTS